Snowflake

Story by Clif Taylor
Illustrations by Anna Whitmire

A Collaborative Publication of  and  Gold Leaf Press

Connected Spirit
Publications

Snowflake by Clif Taylor

Illustrated by Anna Whitmire

A Collaborative Publication of
Connected Spirit Publications, Houston, TX
Gold Leaf Press, Detroit, MI

Cover and book design: Tony Boisvert; Boisvert Design

Editorial Director: Rebecca J. Ensign

Library of Congress Cataloging-in-Publication Data

Taylor, Clif.
   Snowflake / written by Clif Taylor ; illustrated by Anna Whitmire.
       p. cm.
    ISBN-13: 978-1-886769-97-7 (1-886769)
    ISBN-10: 1-886769-97-4
    1. Snowflakes--Juvenile literature. I. Whitmire, Anna, ill. II. Title.
                                                    2010045175
    QC926.37.T39 2010
    551.48--dc22

10987654321

$15.95

ISBN-13: 978-1-886769-97-7
ISBN 10: 1-886769-97-4

Dedication

To my snowflake,
Emma Sofia Taylor

Thank you to

John and Claudia Taylor, Brent Taylor,
Lynn Knisley, Rebecca J. Ensign, Mike Carpenter

Acknowledgments

Kelly Blakley, Jen Weaver-Neist

Snowflake

Story by Clif Taylor
Illustrations by Anna Whitmire

I am a snowflake.

I'm made from a single speck of dust
and ice crystals joined together.

I used to live on a cloud with all my family and friends.

When I got too heavy, I started
falling from the cloud, flying
like a bird, floating with the wind. . .
until I landed gently in the trees,
then on the ground.

No snowflake looks the same.

Snowflakes are all different sizes and shapes.

Children love to have
fun with snowflakes
in many, many ways.

When spring came,
the sun warmed me up and
I turned into a drop of water.

Some of my friends sank into the
ground to give the plants a drink
of water, while the rest of us made
little puddles on top of the ground.

The more the sun warmed us,
the bigger puddles we made.

After a few days, a big rainstorm came.

The wind and rain got stronger, pushing us out of the puddle and into a creek.

The fish in the creek drank some
of us like we were water in a glass.

Just like the wind carries air for
people to breathe, we carry air
with us that fish use to breathe.

When the creek got bigger,
it started moving faster
and we flowed into a river.

The river was big, beautiful, and full of all kinds of new plants and animals.

The best part was all the people.

They liked to swim and play games in the river the same way the children did when we were puddles.

At one point, the river water started moving faster and faster because we started going downhill.

Then we were pushed into a lake.

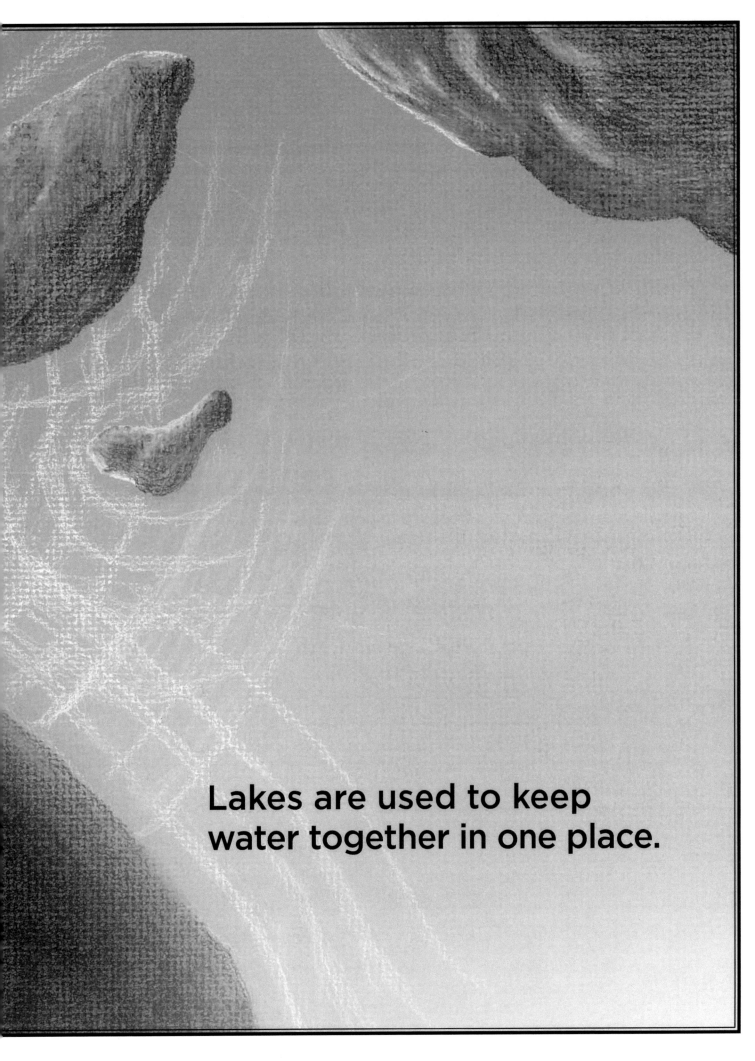

Lakes are used to keep
water together in one place.

The lake had a cove in it where
everyone came to rest and be quiet.

It wasn't too long before we moved out of the cove, back into the main body of the lake.

Not too far up ahead,
I heard a loud rumbling
noise and saw something
I hadn't seen before.

The closer we got to it, the louder the rumbling noise got, and we started moving faster. Before I knew it, we were going as fast as a bullet.

We went through a dam.

A dam holds water back and helps make rivers into lakes.

Dams have giant generators in them that water goes through to make electricity.

After a little while, we slowed down
again and we were back in the river.

Rivers twist and turn, bend and curve, for miles and miles before they reach their end.

Smaller rivers can meet
to make one giant river.

When a river ends, it flows into an ocean or sea.

When a river and an ocean come together, the ocean's salt water goes to the bottom and the fresh river water stays on top.

We flowed into an ocean that was full of new fish, plants, and colors that were different from anything I'd seen before.

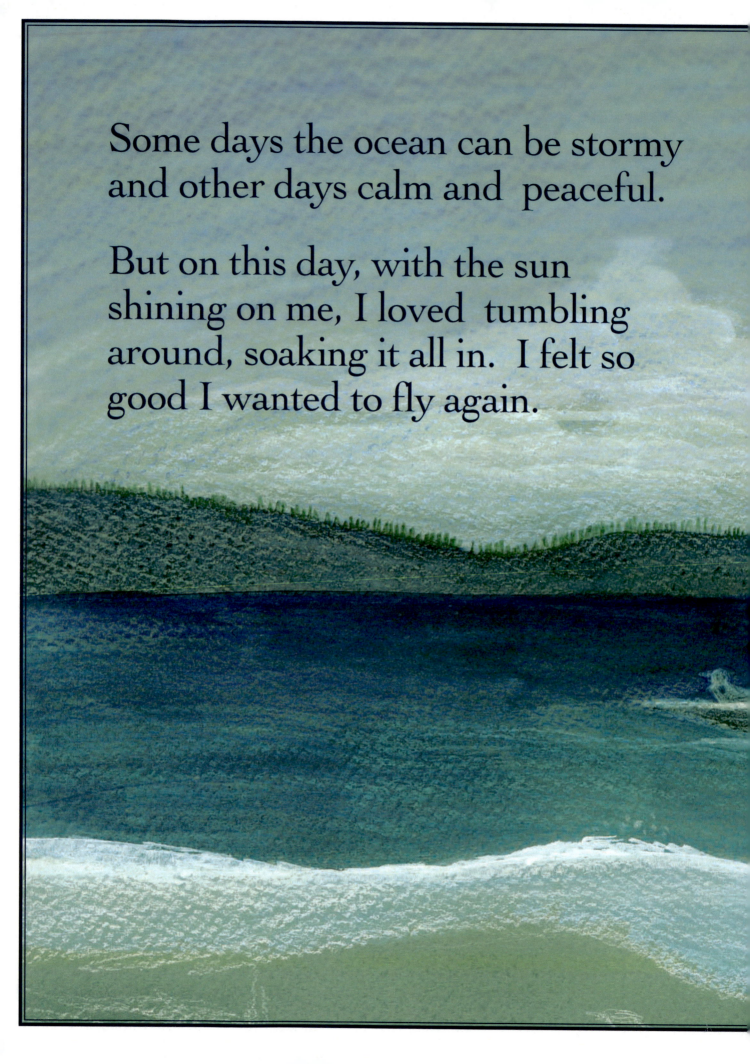

Some days the ocean can be stormy
and other days calm and peaceful.

But on this day, with the sun
shining on me, I loved tumbling
around, soaking it all in. I felt so
good I wanted to fly again.

Then, in an instant,
I was flying again!

"Look at me!" I said.

"I'm going back up into the clouds!"

"Maybe I can be a raindrop or
maybe even a snowflake again."

Some snowflakes have come down from the sky and stayed in the same snow bank for millions of years, frozen the whole time.

Some snowflakes live in clouds that move so fast and high in the sky they go around the whole world in 10 days.

The story of a snowflake is the story of the life cycle of water.

The End

About the Author

Clif Taylor, Author, is a resident of Houston Texas. The father of two sons, Brent and John, Clif also has one daughter in-law, Claudia, and a granddaughter, Emma Sofia – the inspiration for this book's cover. As the author of two non-fiction books, **Connect** and **Awakenings**, Clif draws on the experiences of wonder and intent to inspire readers to learn and live with love. He is humbled and grateful for the opportunity to share the literary works that he has created through his personal experiences.

About the Illustrator

Anna Whitmire, Illustrator, also from Houston, Texas, is an artist, illustrator, and dancer. In love with the great outdoors, she draws her inspiration from anything and everything wild and free. When she is not climbing rocks, singing to the wind, or dancing along pine forest trails, she is in her studio trying to recapture the memories that remain etched in her senses. She is extremely grateful to the various children in her life who constantly refresh her ability to see the world in a youthful and unaffected way. Her hope is that someday, we will all see the world through the eyes of children.

Snowflake is the first in a series of four children's books by Clif and Anna. Also by Clif Taylor and Ann Whitmire: **Oak Tree**, **Raindrop** and **The Bird Alphabet Book**.

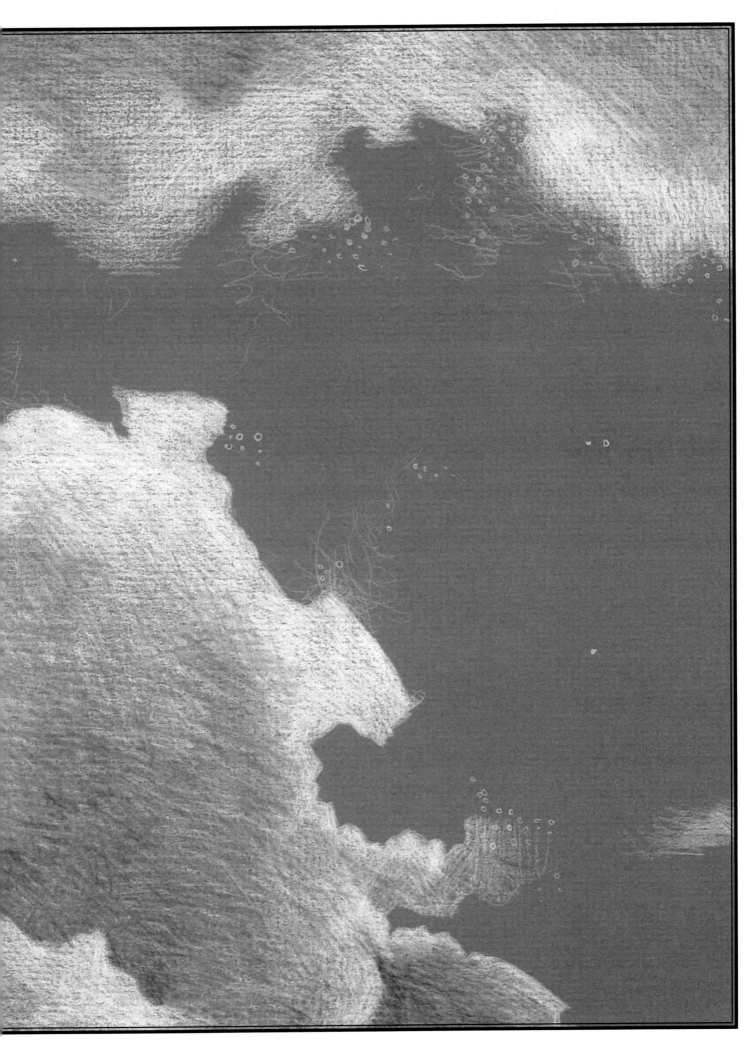